FROZEN HILLS ARE MELTING NOW

A POETRY COLLECTION

MONJIKA D.

To youth

Contents

Contents

"Don't bend; don't water it down;

Don't try to make it logical;

Don't edit your own soul according to the fashion.

Rather, follow your most intense obsessions mercilessly."

FRANZ KAFKA

Foreword

Dear Reader,

Before turning the page, know that every page is different, every poem is another new story so, do not read them like they are siblings, read them like they're a brand new stranger. In context, poetry can be faint, mild or even extremely strong in taste; when you are reading someone's poetry, you are getting to know the sensations they had felt, you are able to communicate and perhaps relate to them; poetry I believe is the most intimate form of art that is meant to be read slowly while savouring every piece of line and most importantly, feeling it as it is.

Monjika D.

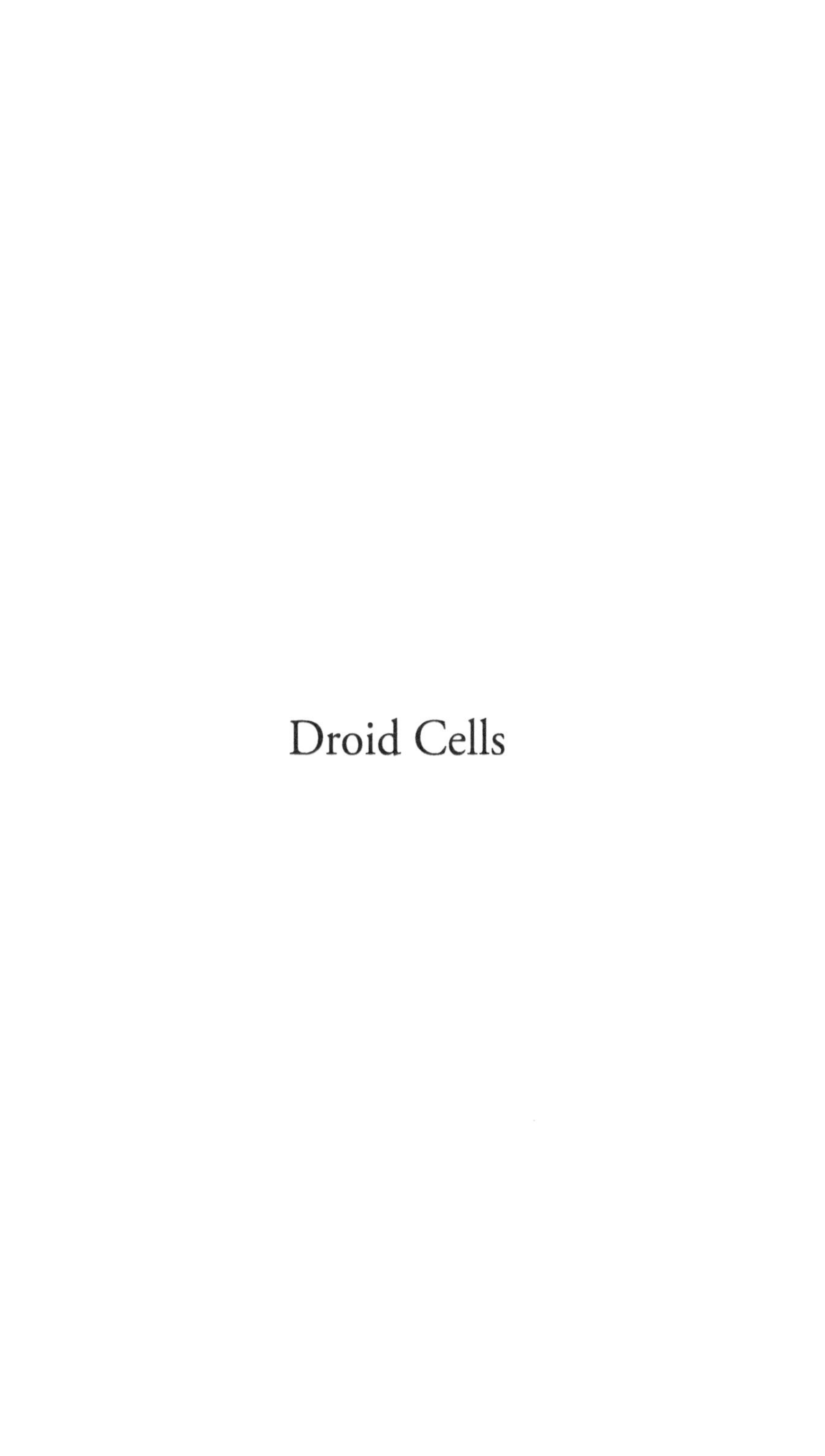

Droid Cells

1. Hearts

I speak of hunger when I chase hope,
I speak of connection when I run to you;
our hearts are not elastic, they bend and snap
but it's true our hearts are starving bastards,
Seldom satisfied.
you can fill your hearts to the brim
and yet, it would seep away
through tiny holes of expectations
and numeral wishes.
you can never fulfil a heart,
it's like a sponge that can suck off everything
and flood you to despair.

2. Adapted

moonlit night sky.
white blue lights
That fades darkness my eyes wait for it,
the round full moon yet to call me.
When will it call?
voices instead,
not-so-sweet,
Their voice was a base of sand silt
always in tempt to drown you,
stony mid layer to take you by surprise
and top glassy layer, sprinkled with nails
ready to stab you as you hear
but, let it in
I want to savour its taste
until I'm adapted.

3. Kill them alone

colourful room, a space, a universe?
blinking lights and dancing bodies
deafening music that possesses these bodies
guides them like a puppet,
even higher when they drink heavenly water
that comes in different hues again.
I look around and I see different colours,
it makes me dizzy but good,
which type of good I don't know;
we all bath in colours as one
our bodies sway like a swing
when we lose our minds, and
I like losing my mind,
it makes this heavy cumbersome body lighter
so much lighter that I swear I could fly,
if not for my dress and heels.
I wanted this moment to last forever
even though it's nothing special
maybe you don't need a special someone
to make things special,
you can kill the night all alone too.

4. Tough still

I feel like my hands are still in a twist,
I want to unleash them from that knot,
let them be free and breath,
but something pulls them back
like a spring and binds them again.
I wish I could be more relaxed,
Why am I so goddamn still?
I guess thats what makes me a cactus,
Can someone take out my spikes?
or maybe I should dry up and lose it all.

5. Noisy head

a human unaligned and imperfect
that strives for perfection
and dreams too high and too much?
a human brain is capable of many things
but can it ever stop thinking?
I wish my brain would stop thinking,
like imagine how it would be
to have a silent mind?
I neither have a silent heart nor a silent mind
all I'm made of is loud chaotic noises.

6. Choices

scarlet windows open into red river,

its maroon glow of whispering delicacies

racks every inch of me with slow shocks

the gravel way to swim in it,

melted into silt the way back

no return! no return.

this wasn't a warning,

it was an ending of line

no choice! no choice

Redesign the heart and mind

Don't worry that your head is screaming

Don't worry that your heart is racing;

Redesign the heart and mind.

Your mind is like a storehouse made of metal

But what if someone made it gold?

Your heart is like an unfiltered sponge unguarded

that's exhaling rawness all naked.

But a golden mind would rot too soon,

So let it be stainless steel, hard to hit.

And a spongy heart shall turn to stone as

Softness dwells hungry pests like mattresses,

So plaster it black and cool it to amber

That's ready to burn anytime.

7. Past

Rome wasn't built in a day
And so was your life today.
Maybe look back a little,
Clear your eyes and focus
Don't fly away from the past,
Just Like how history
made us reconstruct future
Let your past breath a little;
After all, you rose out of it,
Whether bad or good.

8. Jagged

jagged souls
tip-toe steps
mournful eyes
for misery tide
cater to a need
scournful wave,
I strive for excess
excess is what lived!
excess is what killed!
what cures my soul?
nothing holds me still
let me be
let me be

Today Again Tomorrow

9. Everyday

I hate that every day
I wake up to please
In every beads of others.
I hate that everyday
I glamour myself
to hide myself.
I hate that everyday
I say yes to everything
and pretend as if I like it.
I hate that everyday
I smile and lie, so
As to feel I'm okay.
Everyday is telling me
to stretch myself a little more,
Everyday is an act,
cause no one cares otherwise.

10. A sham pearl

I was in search,

for an unreachable thing

called perfection

when someone told me "you are perfect"

but I didn't felt that way,

I was just a sham;

like copper painted gold,

like glistening plastic pearls.

I wanted to be a deep ocean pearl

and so desperately did I pained to believe it

But not everyone can be,

Not everyone is supposed to.

11. I

'I' is a word I can never feel to be mine
I gave up on that word the day I decided
I wanted to be like her;
the girl I never met, nor saw
she wasn't even real, just like me
nor could she ever, but she was someone,
who existed amongst the silent laws of these world,
a deceptive fucking world that I'm manacled to forever.
-some girls after 13

12. Swamp Sea

The gentle lapping of the briny sea water
against the gritty dark sand,
cold bare feet moulded into this
glistening volcanic sand,
vestige of salt in my mouth
and air that feels so sweet.
cries of seagulls flying low and high,
getting ready for a new day's hunt
and the distant horizon cast with
golden light of the rising sun.
I failed again, only to see this sight again
I failed again, only to feel this air again
I failed again, only to be her again
I'm born again empty,
only to be filled with lies again.
I failed to live.

13. Regret

It's as if no ones here to hear me
I found my voice but no one to tell to,
it's like there's a maze in my mind
where I'm lost trying to find,
find the way which you found
but I can never, never.
Should've started doing my own thing
making my own route, then
maybe I wouldn't be in here
cause I'm stuck,
I can't think like you
I'm so stupid;
were not similar
should've thought sooner,
Now I regret, regret.

14. Glimpse

when I was dreaming
I had glimpse of someone,
it was a girl standing still in middle
of a path that ended as it began.
she was dusty and faded
like some old carpet or a rug,
but one which gave no warmth.
she never made a move,
but just gazed at the nothingness
with her hollow eyes.
I knew who she was,
the very girl I was growing into

15. Layers

when I again felt something wrong about me
I instantly painted another coat on my face
then another layer,
it kept getting thicker and thicker
until it got moulded into my face,
like some perfect mask
but, it was so fitted and thick
that I was scared to remove it
so I decided not to,
after all it's a part of me...isn't it?
but at some point even this perfect mask
started to melt like wax.

16. Dig deep

I got my knees deep into this black slit sand
its tiny bead like particles pricking me,
I grab a fistful of them that flows down,
down like white water of the dark seas.
I had pretended to myself that I came for a walk
but now I'm neck deep into this cold
white sea that even though being so bright,
gives no sight of what's beneath.
I dip my head under the water
becoming deaf and mute,
silence in my body
my eyes see the sight
I was never supposed to
but I've seen this twice already.
I go deeper, deeper than the sea itself
I reach the floor of my conscious
but it's still not it, I need to go further
past this barrier of my past,
I need to break it and tear it,
leave this history of me that I never created
but those around, who so eager to ruin me
they who dusted of themselves unto me
and made me become someone I never was

yet...I can't seem to blame them, why?
there was always something wrong with me
I wanted to be everything everyone wants
but in wanting so,
I became a stranger to myself.

Chapter17

Look around and open your ears,
They're all in wait,
Before the storm arrives.
Everyone's in riots and protests,
Marching banners, coloured flags
painted faces of anger and vice,
Stomping loud feets on asphalt roads,
The sky echoing in shouts and cries
They're all fighting and speaking,
Justice, rights, punish, exile, remove!
Uniform men walks in as usual
Some get beaten, some get killed
Hardly do someone care,
Let the top-tier handle?
Smoke, dust, stones and guns,
All in stuporous assert.
Keep looking, don't stop,
They're all in mood to kill
oust the authorities and the orthodox
Who can stop? None.
Both in brew to vanquish the other;
Reminds me of cold war
A vendetta of dominance and power:

We have drowned into a crusade for rights.

Now stop looking,

Your eyes are bleeding.

• 23 •

18. Makeup

They say accept yourself the way you are,
If you wear makeup, remove it and walk bare faced
But, what if you're not hiding and
just being yourself with makeup?
What if you just want to feel pretty
and love the way you look with that makeup?
Then do so, wear that makeup,
colour your lips and eyes
If you feel good that way,
then it's perfectly okay.
Always remember that it's right,
to accept yourself in whatever form you wish to do.

19. Split

Are you seeing it?
Feeling the slow poison?
That's making you split yourself among others?
Watch them and you became them,
Read this or that, and it's engraved in your brain
These years of turmoil,
will definitely cause me brain damage.
My hearts teared enough,
No need of healing,
They'll bring you a new heart?
What the hell is this,
I can't feel any reality or truth.

20. Questions

Are you a hypocrite?

Do you ever just preach of honesty and self-love

And then suddenly feel like wearing that facade of lies?

Do you wish to destroy the mask but yet again hide away?

Are you and me a hypocrite at times?

Is this how we're built?

Can we ever be real and pure?

But that would be dangerous, cause:

Too exposed and you're scratched.

21. Anger under perspectives

Sometimes it's impossible to get angry at someone
Because I've come to the point
where I understand their perspective
And it may seem uncaring
but this is sometimes frustrating
for I wish I could lash out
and simply get rid of my rage.

22. Desire

honey coated body of golden hue,
milk soft hands like cotton delight,
moves like gentle ripples on a lake,
cherubic-glazed copper eyes, and
blue green veins of purple blemished beauty,
you make my ocean tremble in avidity;
your cherry pink lips so prone to bruise
Would I ever be allowed a kiss?
this wild imaginings of a besotted heart
could very well turn tenebrous,
but your muffled voices under my Manus
quells my incessant quests for you.

23. Slaver lover

Halfmoon unreal glazed eyes
Too clear; it pierces my core.
Hear me, raven hair beauty,
Oh, a ravish spirit!
that brings such enrapture;
Enthralling like sorcery.
How many have stopped breathing?
thunderstruck and razor sharp you are,
Your sweep and mass combusts me
And burns me to lurid flames!
This sweetness of agony livid in my flesh,
Trembling frail tendons screaming your name
Only you! only you shall tear my bones apart
And sooth that stretch of my boundless fervour for you.

24. Winter stories

I.

When I am with you, I feel your warmth
the same warmth that has melted away
our love like snow, but what still remains
are the waters I hold onto, and for which I'll wait
till next winter, to be our snow again.

II.

When I first met you,
you were like soft snow
on a Christmas morning
but, now you are just hard blue ice
of the lonely Arctic,
wanting nothing but,
to cut through my love for you.

III.

but at the end,
you were the rains of heaven
that fell to me,
like cold hard hailstones.

25. Menance

to you I go in blessings of dawn
and to you I leave in the curse of dusk,
but to you my love never stops
and no matter what forces meddles,
I am still a greater menace.

26. Ode to your facets

you are meant to be nurtured like an orchid,
you are a rarity in this wacked world
of unsaid and unseen happenings,
you hide underneath leaves of smiles like a mushroom,
and poisonous may you be,
you can fool anyone so I adore.
they envy your mind,
I envy your pretences
you love to act so lovingly,
That some get pulled so lost.
your words are like soft smooth cheese,
they spread swiftly very warm
And brings a salty quiddity in our lives.
your words can be a disguise
that brings hailstones instead of snow
and even your words of warmth
make every soul freeze, why?
you are a sharp blue ice, my love.

27. Artist

I breath into you bloodied lips
Plumped with heat and blood
Your hands runs across my body
Like a artists veering brush
Painting with shades of your love.
You are an artist with no name
And no fame
You are an artist with passion
And desire
And I am your blank canvas.

28. Magenta lips

I say what I say,
Magenta lips of lies
Muddy grave of
White petals strewn
Facade of a rotting beauty
A pit for all to fall.
And yet they flee
Only To fall again.

29. Confetti

You have perforated my heart with so much love
it's too much now.
I do not wish to tremble under you,
it's shaking me apart.
I loved you before the moon went black,
and now I must leave like the dried autumn leaves.
You showed me the sun,
and now it's burning me alive.

Chimeric Visions

30. Mountain goddess

A dusty glassed sky with broken crystal shards,

drawing harlequin hollows into the damp earth.

Pearl beads hung on the dark needles

Of the gnarled crowning pines;

The foggy cool air drenched in sweet aroma

Of barbed crisp pine cones

Whose winged browns rustled spongy wet.

The mountain rain hallowed the land

With green depth and vignette smokes,

Wisps of clouds flattered above like broken feathers

And the tame sun shone in and out like mousy squirrels.

Bird songs echoed at distance behind the black hills

And reclined rock walls, cushioned the fierce water

That fell like uncanny blessings .

It was a white day of remembrance and looks,

Soft dayglow comforted heart's concord,

My body was like a barren rowboat

Gliding across groves and muddy tops

Over the Himalayas, Fuji, Rocky's, Tianmen and Denali!

I sailed slow and good, for the ripples of love and joy

Bestrewed me into euphoric waves and parallels.

Oh! thee mountain goddess,

You never fail to jolt the senses out,

Like a stupefying callum
Yet, bridled with blight.

31. Face

cracked chalk mouth,
in tributary of blood
dappled with dust
talking in dirt;
It was a face in the realm of faces
similar but in cryptic dearth,
waiting to be stamped flat?
waiting for one to see and then vanish?
What was its purpose?
I stood ground watching it
slightly perplexed, when
everything blurred in to a focal point
with that face in radical aura
its eyes were on me
and my eyes on it
a deliberative drawl of presence
and anticipation
useless one at that;
it smiled ghoulishly
red water trickling down its morbid face
and pooled beneath in a tranquil muddle.

32. Butterfly

I wish to be a butterfly
flying all day, sucking on
Sweet juices of pretty flowers
On a sunny blue day.
and I wouldn't care
if I am to be hurt
since butterflies don't feel pain.
And when it gets dark
I would go hide under a leaf
Or crawl deep between
blades of grass or
into a cervice of a rock
with my wings wrapped
Tightly around me,
And wait until I fall asleep.
I wish to be like a butterfly that dies
after a short but beautiful life of no pain.

33. Odd hours Oddness

this body is my form
this form is my body
but this body is a vessel,
a vessel of my existence
existence is state of being present
and living is a state of being alive,
but lack of life is death
not living, is a state of being dead.
when you are eating or drinking
laughing or crying
walking or running
thinking or believing
singing or dancing
waking or sleeping
you are living;
those are ways of proving that you're alive
but when humans stop doing those things
They are termed as being dead.
however there is way of being dead without being dead
It's called being empty;
when you lose any meaning or purpose
you become empty
like an empty vessel,

your heart is beating
brain is working
body is functioning
but your soul is trapped,
or maybe trying to escape.
when you become empty
they think you are sad,
but sadness is like a pain.
when you are sad
you are feeling something
but when you are empty,
you are not feeling anything
nor sad nor happy
just nothing.
the feeling of emptiness cannot be described
cause being empty is not feeling
so, how does one describe this thing
When they ask "how are you feeling, tell me?"

34. Dizzy

Blue spider webs hung on high ceilings,
Glazy wide gaps drooling of dusty clouds,
Old chick house and abandoned farms
This odd shack drips in dried paint
And blooded walls of slaughtered pigs
I remember this morbid dream;
And I was its main course dish
Being sliced and bathed in sauce
Too hot gravy and a pig head beside,
Its pointy long snout and jaw hung opened,
Teeths pulled out and skin off,
Dressed only in tomatoes, coriander and spice.
A strange curiosity came over
And I launched upon the faceless chef
He stumbled down and with little struggle
Vanished in thin air,
The pig was not longer there,
It came alive running towards exit
But there was no door or window.
Two steps I took
And fell down a void
Floating weightless
pig nowhere in sight.

I opened my eyes
And found myself in a dinner table
On some occasion I forgot,
Mom asked "would you like some more?"
I looked at the slice of pig meat
And nodded involuntarily,
and when I was served.
I ate and savoured it full.
-useless

35. Ruins

High steps up to the hill of ruins,
Old, dusty and dirty
A climb that dries your lungs
And as you reach the top,
You're left heaving and gasping.
I look up and see the red sky,
Two burning ball of fire on either side
Wisps of white clouds vaporising slowly
I look down and see the green plain,
Flat full of vegetation
Various trees, orchards and lots of dandelions
Floating away into the cool summer wind.
Far beyond there is the tranquil sea,
Full of rocks and boathouses.
And suddenly, the wind speeds up
Clouds turn dark and sullen,
The sky goes whirling and sun goes black
Like fire wood cooling into charcoal.
The land beneath me shakes; violent
I have nothing to hold onto.
Should I shout for help?
No one would hear me up so high,
Should I go down?

But I would fall.

End